Summer

LABURNUM PRESS

Stephen White-Thomson

LABURNUM PRESS

Laburnum House Educational Ltd.
Caldicott Drive
Heapham Road Industrial Estate
Gainsborough
DN21 1FJ

British Library Cataloguing in Publication Data (CIP) exists for this title.

ISBN: 978 1 9098 5049 1

Printed in China through World Print Ltd
Printed on chlorine-free paper from sustainably managed sources

Developed and created for Laburnum Press by

White-Thomson Publishing Ltd
www.wtpub.co.uk

Acknowledgements:
Educational consultant: Kate Ruttle
Picture research: Stephen White-Thomson
Proof reader: Izzi Howell
Designer: Clare Nicholas

Contents

Summer heat

Phew I'm hot!

I love it when it's hot in the summer!

I pant when

I am hot.

What do you do?

5

Keeping cool

When we drink water, it keeps us cool.

6

Woof!

Dogs splash in water to keep cool.

7

Summer fun

Where would you put up a tent?

What can you do in a park near you?

Let's go to the Coast!

On sunny days, we like to go to the seaside.

Cycling in woods is fun – and cool!

How many strawberries

can you see here?

sticky!

Why do ice creams

melt in the sun?

Eating outside

We like cooking food

on barbecues.

sizzle!

16

Which picnic food do you like to eat?

17

Summer clothes

sandals →

What clothes do you like ...

19

Summer plants

ripe

unripe

Tomatoes are a summer fruit.

What can you make from

these sunflowers?

Sparklers books are designed to support and extend the learning of young children. Regular winners of Practical Pre-School silver and gold awards, the books' high-interest subjects link to the Early Years curriculum and beyond. Find out more about Early Years foundation stages (EYFS) at www.gov.uk/government/publications/early-years-foundation-stage-framework–2, and reading with children from the National Literacy Trust (www.literacytrust.org.uk).

Themed titles
Summer is one of four **Seasons** titles that encourage children to learn about the fun and informative aspects of their lives in the different seasons. The other titles are **Winter** (ISBN: 978 1 9098 5051 4), **Spring** (ISBN: 978 1 9098 5048 4) and **Autumn** (ISBN: 978 1 9098 5050 7)

The prime areas of learning: (taught in nurseries)
- communication and language
- physical development
- personal, social and emotional development

The specific areas of learning: (taught in reception classes)
- literacy
- mathematics
- understanding the world
- expressive arts and design

Making the most of reading time
When reading with younger children, take time to explore the pictures together. Ask children to find, identify and count or describe different objects. Point out colours and textures. Allow quiet spaces in your reading so that children can ask questions or repeat your words. Try pausing mid-sentence so that children can predict the next word. This sort of participation develops early reading skills.

Follow the words with your finger as you read. The main text is in Infant Sassoon, a clear, friendly font designed for children learning to read and write. The label and sound effects add fun and give the opportunity to distinguish between levels of communication. Where appropriate, labels, sound effects or main text may be presented phonetically. Encourage children to imitate the sounds.

As you read the book, you can also take the opportunity to talk about the book itself with appropriate vocabulary such as "page", "cover", "back", "front", "label" and "page number".

You can also extend children's learning by using the books as a springboard for discussion and further activities. There are a few suggestions on the facing page.

Pages 4–5
Talk about colours that make you feel warm or hot (usually reds, oranges and yellows). Make a 'hot' collage of colours cut or torn out of catalogues and magazines. Count how many times you see these colours today.

Pages 6–7
Children may like to make cocktail stick ice-lollies in different flavours to see which one they like the taste of. Use an ice-cube tray and pour small amounts of different drinks into each section. Pop in a cocktail stick, put the tray in the freezer and wait. While you wait, ask your child what they think will happen to the drinks. After a few hours, find out if they were right. Which drink was best as an ice-lolly?

Pages 8–9
If you can, take your child to a park; otherwise look at picture or videos of people in parks. Try to develop your child's use and understanding of words that describe where people and things are or where they are going, for example "*up*", "*in*", "*under*", "*through*", "*beside*".

Pages 10–11
What is the man putting on the little girl's nose? Can your child tell you why? Talk about the importance of keeping safe in the sun. Draw a picture of a child like yours and ask your child to suggest ways of dressing the picture-child. Cut out a sun hat and long-sleeved top and ask your child to dress the picture-child for being in the sun.

Pages 12–13
Children may enjoy a visit to the woods. Even if you can't cycle, it's a cool place to be on a hot day. Take a magnifying glass, paper and crayons for drawing what you see. Encourage your child to stay still for long enough to look carefully for small things in the woods, such as ladybirds.

Pages 14–15
How many things can your child count? Put one ball of blu-tak on each of the strawberries. Encourage your child to put a finger on each blu-tak ball to squash it as they count it. How many can they count? If they can count to 10, try some simple addition with your blu-tak balls e.g. "I have 3 balls. If I add two more, how many balls will I have?"

Pages 16–17
Your child may like to help you to make a simple fruit salad using delicious summer fruits. Always supervise children with knives. Teach your child how to hull a strawberry; talk about the different smells of oranges, raspberries and peaches. Can your child identify a fruit with their eyes closed, just by smelling it?

Pages 18–19
Can your child dress themselves in their favourite summer clothes? How long does it take? Use a timer to time them dressing themselves in different summer outfits. Help them to think about the order they put their clothes on. Perhaps they can get themselves ready quicker if they put their clothes in order first?

Pages 20–21
Has your child seen a bird feeder? Show them one, and have a look at the seeds (if your child has a nut allergy, they should wear gloves as a precaution). Use tweezers to sort them into groups of 'the same kind of seed'. Count how many groups you make. What will you do with them now? Make a picture or give the seeds to the birds?

Index

Picture acknowledgements:
Shutterstock: cover (mimagephotography) 4 (SkillUp), 5 (Mat Hayward),
6 (D. Hammonds), 7 (Tania Katsai), 8 (Goodluz), 12 (smereka), 15 (Lori Sparkia),
17 (wavebreakmedia), 18–19 (Sergey Novikov), 20 (Cristina Annibali); **Thinkstock**:
4 (Thomas Nortcut), 9 (Bec Parsons), 10 (Windzepher), 11 (travnikovstudio),
13 (gorillaimages), 14 (amanamiagesRF), 16 (Purestock), 21 (Ale-ks).
Background to 2, 3, 22, 23, 24 is Thinkstock/connect11.